FROM SHA

TO LIGHT

Poems of a Grieving Man

FROM SHADOWS TO LIGHT

Poems of a Grieving Man

John Toso, MD

Speedwell Press

To my dear Joann Marie

From Shadows to Light: Poems of a Grieving Man
John Toso, MD

Photo credits: Brenden Simonson and John Toso; Shutterstock

CONTENTS

ACKNOWLEDGMENTS

I must give thanks to Belita Schindler and Meridee Ofstedahl for sharing their copy of Martha Whitmore Hickman, Healing after Loss, HarperCollins, New York, 2002; and to Belita for providing me a copy of Jane Yolen, Things to Say to a Dead Man, Holy Cow! Press, Duluth, 2011.

These two books have shaken me out of my stupor and have started the creative juices to run. This has been a cathartic journey in sharing my widower's journey into the strange country of grief.

Other resources from which I have benefited during this journey are the following:

- Sheldon Vanauken, *A Severe Mercy*, HarperCollins, 1977
- Joyce Rupp, *Praying Our Goodbyes*, Ave Maria Press, 1988
- Kara Tippetts, *The Hardest Peace*, David C. Cook, 2014

All quotes from the Holy Bible, unless otherwise noted, are from the New International Version, New York International Bible Society, Zondervan, 1982.

I must also thank my dear friends Tim Rietz, MD, Mark Monson, MD, the late Rev. Dr. Ron Jensen, Kathryn Colestock-Burke, Barbara Nelson and Cynthia Griffin who have been my faithful and patient readers, encouraging me on my way.

I would be remiss if I did not give credit to my high school mission-school teacher—the late Rev. Ted Berkas—who challenged us in composition, English and poetry with a passion that has endured in his students to this day.

Finally, I thank my Savior who has never been far away. Well acquainted with grief, He continues to sustain me from day to day.

PREFACE

A month or so after losing Joann, my wife of forty two years and my life-long friend, I received two books in the mail from Belita Schindler, a dear friend who had tragically lost her husband two years earlier. Another widow in the community had given her the first book, *Healing After Loss: Daily Meditations for Working Through Grief*, by Martha Whitmore Hickman. Both had used this book, regularly adding generous penciled comments and stars in the margins.

The second book, *Things to Say to a Dead Man: Poems at the End of a Marriage and After*, by Jane Yolen was new with a few key pages marked by Belita. When asked she said that she did not want the books back. They were now mine on which to work. These two women have processed the first years of their grief and are moving on in their respective journeys.

I have found Jane Yolen's collection of poems to be especially poignant, reflecting experiences in my own grief process. I have decided that a counterpoint of poems from the widower's perspective would complement her sharing. If you hear echoes of either of these two books in my collection, you are not mistaken. I hope this will aid you as you work through your own distinctive journey of grief.

A rough chronology of my wanderings after my wife's death might help to understand the flow of this collection of poems:

- Immediate pre- and post-death musings
- A cruise to 'Down Under' within a week of her death to join my two brothers and wives on a trip that had been previously booked
- Memorial service upon return from the cruise
- Move to new condo
- RV trip to the Southwest with my brother
- Solo travel to Madagascar, Tanzania, France and the UK to visit past missionary posts, friends, and family
- Transition to a new life and eventually a new relationship

Years ago in high school I played the part of the Stage Manager in Thornton Wilder's *Our Town*. The role of a poet is so well put in this snippet from the play:

> *Emily:* Oh, Mama, look at me one minute as though you really saw me. Mama, fourteen years have gone by. I'm dead. You're a grandmother, Mama! Wally's dead, too. His appendix burst on a camping trip to North Conway. We felt just terrible about it - don't you remember? But, just for a moment now we're all together. Mama, just for a moment we're happy. Let's really look at one another!...I can't. I can't go on. It goes so fast. We don't have time to look at one another. I didn't realize. So all that was going on and we never noticed. Take me back -- up the hill -- to my grave. But first: Wait! One more look. Good-bye, Good-bye world. Good-bye, Grover's Corners....Mama and Papa. Good-bye to clocks ticking.... and Mama's sunflowers. And food and coffee. And new ironed dresses and hot baths....and sleeping and waking up. Oh, earth, you are too wonderful for anybody to realize you. Do any human beings ever realize life while they live it—every, every minute?
>
> *Stage Manager:* No. (pause) The saints and poets, maybe they do some.
>
> *Emily:* I'm ready to go back.

PART ONE: SHADOWS TO DARKNESS

"This is the Hour of Lead—
Remembered, if outlived,
As freezing persons recollect the Snow—
First Chill—then Stupor—then letting go."
Emily Dickinson

"The sun shall be turned to darkness."
Joel 2:31

"My heart is anguish within me;
The terrors of death have fallen upon me."
Psalm 55:4

"If today was not a crooked highway,
If tonight was not a crooked trail,
If tomorrow wasn't such a long time,
Then lonesome would mean nothin' to you at all.

Yes'n if only my own true love was waitin'
And I could only hear her heart a'softly poundin',
Yes'n if only she was lying by me,
Then I'd lie in my bed once again."
Bob Dylan

LOOSE HOLD

I'm home from another day's emergency shift,
With just enough time to grab a bite to eat.
Off to the hospital to check on your progress
In one of your countless brushes with death.

Off the elevator to the sixth floor,
I check your room, you are not there. I inquire:
"Where is my wife, has she been moved?"
"She is down the next hall in ICU."

ICU!! I race down the hall;
Already there, our daughter and your mother,
Your body is tilted down ten degrees, head down,
Your color is ashen and you are barely aware.

Alarms spell out what is already obvious,
Your pressure is low and your pulse racing.
I warned them of your risk of hemorrhage,
Now a bit late they chase the tail.

Although ashen your face is serene.
Is this your ticket home?
You have nothing to fear, you are going home.
Lee is right! You have a loose hold on life.

"TSY MISY HEVITRA"

The mastectomy had only given her a few months respite.
This Malagasy lady was again overcome
A chest reeking of nodular cancerous flesh.
Looking at me for hope all I could utter was
"*Tsy misy hevitra.*" (I have no other thoughts.)
Displaying no ill will, but without delay
She and her family were on their way home.

Your bone marrow enemy waited ever so patiently.
Seventeen years of treatments
Kept your enemy at check until
Checkmate! Now lymphoma as well.
R-CHOP chemo is killing your enemy and you
Not slowly....very surely.
You would fight for me to the bitter end,
Yet, this time I must release you.
As Lee often said and is right,
"Your personal hold on this earth is light."

I look at you after a tearful embrace
Cradling your bald pate and decimated frame,
Yet to no degree has faded
Your faith and ready smile.
A quiet agreement, it is time to call hospice.
Is this our "*Tsy misy hevitra*"?
We start preparing our home.
Let's go for a wheelchair ride to see the leaves!

WHERE ARE YOU NOW?

The last I saw you was handing off
Your cool gray still figure
To the University Bequeathal team.
They closed our bedroom door
And fifteen minutes later
Your body rolled out the bedroom door
Zipped in the proverbial black body bag
On an immaculate chromed gurney
With the team bidding us a subdued goodbye and thank you.

So, where are you now?
Their estimate is eight to eighteen months
Before I get the call to collect your ashes.

Are you on a stainless steel anatomy tray?
Resting in a static formaldehyde-scented recess till the next day's session,
When up from below your corpse will again arise
To the eyes and hands of your assigned doctors-to-be.
They will start on your axillae and then on from there.
What will they find?
Surprise, no spleen! Mayo took that.
Have they given you a nickname?
We named ours 'Freddie'.
So strange! You are just blocks away,
But I will never again see you, hear your laugh,
Hug you good morning, kiss you goodnight,
This side of the sod.

Are you in the arms of your Redeemer?
Or does that wait a rest in peace,
Till we join Him in eternity
Together again?

SUNLIGHT

It was a cloudy May day, the day we wed in Eau Claire.
Thunderstorms rained down on the ski-slope roofed church
Until which time we said our vows
And the sun broke out and filled the sanctuary
With sunlight.
Baraka, Blessing, Sodrano!

It was a dreary day three days before you left.
I could do nothing right.
Cutting words with my only recourse being
Survival.
Was it morphine induced?
Was it demonic?
Then the next day you awoke full of joy.
Sunlight filled the fall colors of the vibrant maples.
Come my love, let's go for a walk!
Your baby sister and I pushed you in your wheelchair
Up the hill to Fulham Street and reveled in the crimson maple leaves.

Your last day was gray
Matching the color of your countenance in those final hours.
My clinical acumen watched the veil slowly fall;
Your eyes now fixed,
Your breathing now erratic.
Suddenly the sun burst into the bedroom window
And you breathed your last.
As you entered into the eternal bliss
Where you will dwell in His light.

FAIRY TALES

"Once upon a time"
This baby girl attended my infant baptism at
L'Église de St. Etienne, Paris, France!
How many times did I take that picture off the wall
To show our beginnings,
The stuff that makes fairy tales.
Then on to growing up together in Madagascar,
You a Montague and me a Capulet.
Taking two shy years to even hold hands.

Then the tale moves on to the romantic words "I do",
Then on to a "very, very fine house"
(But only one cat in the yard.)
We raised our babies
In the "Mother Earth News" house in the woods.

Then off to travel the world, now raising global children.
Then with the word "C"
The fairy tale stopped,
The picture is off the wall.
We did not "live happily ever after".

"AS YOU LIKE IT" [NOT!]

How unusual, you and me
To share the same stage
For all seven stages of life—together.
And so we must
End "this strange eventful history"
'Sans' a lot, but surely not 'oblivion'.
So there, Shakespeare!
So there, Miss Rorstad!

One night before the curtains closed
You slid beneath the sheets 'sans' everything
Even knowing the coming pain of a dried body,
You would give all again to me.

No! This cannot be!
Our last stage call, our last bow
Must be—a tearful embrace.
That must do
Till the lights are out.

CASTING CROWNS

"You want me to go on a Barrier Reef cruise?
So soon after she has died?
What will others say?"
"Can you give us a reason why not to go?"

You two couples and I head for dinner.
"Are we waiting for one more?"
The extra setting begs the question.
This only said once and the steward scurries off with our orders.

Back to the stateroom,
I open the sliding door to the promenade deck
For yet another stunning sunset.
Golden rays dance like diamonds on the swells below.

'Casting down their golden crowns across the glassy sea.'
"Are you with the cherubim and the seraphim
Casting down your crown at your Redeemer's feet?"

My tears join the infinite saline bath below the deck.
Here in a mirror dimly
But then clearly
I will praise Thee face to face.

HONKING GOOSE ON THE LOOSE

Dear one,
I reach to you for advice
You have lost a spouse—your dearest friend.
How have you transitioned from being a couple
To being the odd one out?
You have been my wife's dearest friend seemingly forever,
So you are a rare one in the know.

By now you have read my cruise posts.
What a strange place to play out these early days of loss!
Everywhere screams of vintage folks
Walking the promenade deck or sharing lounge chairs—side by side.
I feel cheated!
I feel like a lone lost Canada goose honking for his mates.

Halfway through this cruise I already tire of the litany of gourmet meals,
The daily three-mile walks on the deck, the nightly entertainment.
But what caps my days as nothing else are
The longing views to endless sea at the bow,
Tropical winds blow through my hair as I hold the rail
To keep me upright in the blast of the tropical wind in my face.
The waning gold of the sunset glistens on the waves below,
I then spot parallel to me
A lone albatross flying as if my wingman.

What I fear is the finality of her memorial awaiting us on our return.
But now, how about you?
How is your mom? Your dog?
Your countdown to retirement?

Affectionately, your honking goose on the loose,
John

PRESENCE

God came near
As our children shared His Word.
Then your dear heart
Spoke of the heavenly golden bowl
Full of your prayers yet to be answered.
As our daughter sang of blind trust
The organ hinted of His presence
In which you now stand!

Yes, God has dealt with death
So that we all have a future:
You, now cradled in His bosom;
And me, for a while, under His wing of grace.
Yea, come Lord Jesus!

MEANING WELL

"How are you doing?" (brief slightly awkward hug)
"I'm doing OK."
"Sorry we missed her memorial,
We were on vacation in Florida."
"If there is anything we can do, anything!
You just call!"
"Thank you, that's kind of you."

"Hey, we should get together sometime,
Go out for pizza and beer."
"Yeah, that'd be a good idea."
"Good to talk to you!
See you around."

HOLY PLACES

Where is it to which I am drawn?
Where I can stop and drink in
The wind, the waves, the gulls
Floating on the currents above?
Is it not to our holy places?

Park Point beach sitting on a beach log
Looking north over the Great Gitche Gumee,
Artist Point, Grand Marais, the long walk to the lighthouse.
Cascade River Gorge, watching the tannin-stained waters flow.
Then upward once again to Lookout Mountain,
Reaching our pulpit rock and look!
A bald eagle gliding suddenly shoots vertical!
Just for you.
I weep for joy.

Sitting at the Cascade Lodge diner
Now without you, sipping pale ale.
Before ending this pilgrimage I walk
Across the road to the bleached Adirondack chairs.
Opening the collected piles of 'In Memory of You' cards.
Now's an OK time to weep freely. I'm not alone…

"Take as long as you wish.
Can you share these kind words with me?
Take time to heal.
This is our holy place."

FIRST CHRISTMAS WITHOUT YOU

Christmas, Emmanuel, God with us.
Yes, God, you must hold us together.
This first fractured Christmas
Holding on to traditions we gather as family
Once again, but without a tree.

Christmas, Emmanuel, God with us.
We read once again Luke chapter 2.
However, no youngster amongst us to read
And you to give them the needed prompts.
A few carols sung, then presents to open.

Christmas, Emmanuel, God with us.
We gather around the table
To share vegan & non-vegan alike;
Grandma's *yulekake* spread with butter;
Fruit soup, *lefse, krumkake* and almond butter balls.

Christmas ornaments, reflections of years together
Now are divided and shared
To be starters for new family Christmas trees.
We all share a hug and wish each well;
Yet all feeling the intense loss of your presence.
Comforted that this Christmas is your first
Christmas with Emmanuel, God with you!

TO TOUCH AND SHARE

I lie in bed, the night-light glows warm yellow.
The room so quiet I hear this pen glide.
I write this poem as a sorry attempt
To once again share my day with you.

I lie in bed, your pillow awaiting you.
The queen bed once barely room enough
For your thrashing feet, now a vast space.

I miss you so, your touch,
The smell of your shampoo in your hair,
Your goose-bumps as I caress your ears,
Holding you with a kiss goodnight.

Then after a few moments of embrace
Our weary bodies would find their familiar positions
Each assured by touch,
Reconciled to share another day,
Until that day the music died.

"FOR ALL WE KNOW"

Can't sleep! Another 2 AM.
Another TPT fund raiser...but wait!
An anthology on 'The Carpenters' to drag me in.

"We've Only Just Begun"
Flashback to Ne-So-Dak Bible Camp
Visiting you in the fall after campers gone.
My red Pontiac Catalina's cassette player
Belting out "For All We Know" as we swoon
Cradling our Budweisers like two naughty kids
Full of new love...then,

"I'll Say Goodbye to Love,
There are no tomorrows for this love of mine."
Tightening of diaphragm and throat followed by
Deep sobs and a well of tears...then...NO, now!

"Love, Look at the Two of Us
Strangers in Many Ways."
My heart aches to fill the void,
To share, to chat, to pray,
To snuggle with our naked bodies front to back,
Too early for us,
"Yet love may grow for all we know."

GRASPING

Shortly after you were gone
The presence of your things
Was too much to bear
Easier to bag them up
For someone else to share.

Our wedding rings
Are now together safe
But never again
On the fingers they belonged.
Our pictures of us together
Down to one on the shelf.

At first this seemed the thing to do
To limit the sobs and ache that came.
Yet now nine months have passed
I find myself going back to photos
And reading Kathryn's powerful memorial
In order to grasp at something, anything,
To feel close to you again.

Even if these memories bring tears
At least I feel that I am somewhat alive.
An ache is better than numb.
Strange that first it felt that
The quicker I got over this thing called grief
That I would be alive again;
Only to find that it doesn't work that way.
Grief will have its toll, will play itself out,
For how long, only God knows.

Time to turn off the lights and phone,
Turn on the stereo, close my eyes,
Play "Bridge over Troubled Waters"
Bringing me back to the very room
Where I first played this to you,
Very young lovers--

Then I will sleep.

GYMNOPEDIE MORNING

Awakened by thunder early this Sunday morning,
I sang a pastoral solo at church
Quite aware you are not there to hear.

Home again for another solo lunch
I turn on 'Pandora' radio--
Another rainy day to share
With Eric Satie's *Gymnopedie #1*
To set the mood--quiet, simple, sweet sadness.

The raindrops course their way
Down the sliding door screen.
Your flower pot shelving stands empty.
I hope today for 'red at night'
Both a sailor's and a widower's delight!

1ère GYMNOPÉDIE

JEALOUSY

As I grew in professional skills and responsibilities
You grew in spiritual depth and maturity.
I only now understand my reticence in attempting a prayer life
To which you yearned for us.
You found that avenue of need in 'Moms in Prayer'.
Yes, only now I see it was jealousy!
I was jealous of a God that held you so close,
Keeping me from joining in spiritual discipline, busy in work.
Now that you are gone and only now
Do I exercise the discipline of devotions,
Morning and evening with Spurgeon* and the Word.
Why only now do I enjoy this revelation
That could have been ours for years!
I am so sorry! Forgive me!

---

*Charles Spurgeon, *Morning And Evening, A Devotional Classic for Daily Encouragement,* Hendrickson Publishers, 1991

THE WALK

Remember our walks together
No phones allowed,
Our kids home with assignments.
Just the dogs and we
Would walk the same path
Sorting out the day
And our future together.
Friends along the way
Would stop and say hello
We would exchange pleasantries
Their dog would sniff ours
And we would be on our way.
Holding hands was the usual,
However, in special moments
We would lock our waists
With our bodies now joined at the hips.

Now without you some discipline
Demands a modicum of routine.
My walk is much the same
Usually the same path
In destination and speed.
Without you by my side
I feel somewhat invisible.
No one recognizes me
But for an occasional polite hello.
Couples still walk their dogs
Stopping to chat with neighbors.
Children ride their bikes
Steering clear of this suspicious man.
It would have been less awkward
If I indeed was invisible.

A cardinal chips in the overhead maple
I call back and then sudden tears
Fill my eyes as I remember

Our many birding walks together,
Remember our delight to find a new one
And then check it off in our bird atlas.
I've got to hurry, wipe the tears!
A couple is coming up the street.
It is easier to remain invisibly boring
Than to accept the polite regret
Of a stranger to a stranger.

My walks without you
Are now more inward than visible.
"My thoughts are many miles away"
As we used to hear Paul Simon sing.
Remember our walks
Our plans for the future
Now sadly gone away.
So, my dear, I will finish this walk
Still believing that there will be
Another day not here but there
Where we will walk again hand in hand
Confident that the future
Will be a forever that we are promised
To share together.

DYSPHORIA

It is now six months since you slipped away
Spring is in full bloom—the 'lovely month of May.'
I hardly dare peek at the bedside clock
As I am fully awake—ready for coffee and start of another day.
However, my clock is as unfriendly as
The first cock's crow in Madagascar,
Heralding two in the morning—and all is NOT well.

I feel a daily constriction in my throat now for weeks,
As if something is stuck!
No help from food or drink—just there.
My doctor mind runs through the well-trained list.
Full sensing an ongoing year of loss and hurt
That this is most likely "globus hystericus,"
That is, "It's all in my head."
However, the litany of possibilities always ends in:
"Is it cancer for me too? Will I join you soon?"
"Will I proverbially die of a broken heart?"

Finally, I succumb to a visit to my doctor
Who properly orders the scope down the gullet--just in case.
She likely agrees this is globus but orders it anyway to assuage my fear.
If it's cancer the thought comes to mind—I have enough meds--
Your palliative meds to send me quickly home to you.
That way I won't put anyone walking that rocky road with me.
I awake from my propofol haze to the words, "All is well."
I was right—it is all in my head. Deal with it!

GET A GRIP!

Years of caring for you
Have taken their toll.
I refuse to succumb
To another waist size up!
Blood pressure is marginally controlled
With two medications.
'Sleepus interruptus' is the norm.

After all the trips to the ER with you
Who will be there for me?
Who will drive me home?
Who do I call at my mid-night crisis?
I'll drop dead before I buy a 'Med-Alert' necklace!

"I worry about you, brother!
When are you going to sign up for the gym again?"

Get a grip, John!

PHYSICIAN, HEAL THYSELF

Back from vacation I walk into the exam room,
"How's George been doing?"
        "He's DEAD! How dare you!"
Oops, time to start reading the obits after a return to town.

Judy, in hospice, dying of ovarian cancer
No family, she's alone, the nurses swamped.
Returning across the street
I cradle my auto-harp
And sing hymns to Judy.
Just Judy and me until it was
Just me.

"Jim, how are things?
It has been a few months now since Joyce has passed.
I am sure the last casserole has been delivered,
Your family has returned to the east coast."

"Jim, you appear to be suffering from more than grief.
Could you be depressed?
Let's talk about it."

Now the table is turned.
I am no longer the professional observer.
Have I seen enough to know myself?
Can I ever be observant enough to heal myself?
Or have we been deluded all along?
For the ultimate healing belongs to Him.

KEEPING TIME

B.C—Before Christ
Then through Him all time changed.
A.D.—Anno Domini—in the year of our Lord,
Until He comes again.

While together, we celebrated—
Birthdays and anniversaries
With cards, flowers, breakfast donut parties;
Hugs, kisses, then finding our familiar curves.
We lived in timeless bliss,
Rarely pondering our future or counting the days,
Till your A.D.—your Anno Domini.

Now all is changed,
A.S.—Anno Solo—the year alone.
I long to return to comfortable routines,
Timeless rituals,
When we lived in abandon
Not counting the time.

I need to move on.
I get it—it's not my Anno Solo
It never was!
A.D.—this is yet the year of our Lord
Until He comes again.

MOTHER'S DAY

Another holiday dilemma—
What to do this Mother's Day?

My mom long gone and now you
The mother of our precious three.
Tanzanite jewelry hidden in the safe
A planned gift for you this day,
Will wait, but for who?
Not this Mother's Day.

I had a knack of outfitting you
Remember that blue dress from Macys?
Now that credit card sits quietly in the safe
Awaiting a purchase, but not for
This Mother's Day.

Each holiday or birthday
We would stop at Target
For yet another greeting card.
To you, a must, like flowers.
Then you were off to Jackie's
To get your hair done up
For Mother's Day.

How strange to endure this holiday
Left only with a picture of you
In that blue Macy's dress and gorgeous hair
On Mother's Day.

PART TWO: WANDERINGS IN THE NIGHT

And I say, "Oh, that I had wings like a dove!
I would fly away and be at rest;
Yes, I would wander far away;
I would lodge in the wilderness."
Psalm 55: 6-7

"I do not know where I am going
or what I will do when I get there.
I know only that to put one foot
in front of the other, moves me on,
away from you to a place,
where I do not want to be."
Jane Yolen

"I can't see my reflections in the water,
I can't speak the sounds to show no pain.
I can't hear the echo of my footsteps,
Or remember the sounds of my own name.
Yes'n if only my own true love was waitin'
And I could only hear her heart a'softly poundin',
Yes'n if only she was lying by me,
Then I'd lie in my bed once again."
Bob Dylan

PAPER TRAILS

Five months since you departed
I finally am sorting through a year's worth of papers and receipts
Evidence that I have been in survival mode for too long.
But now it is tax time—what better motivation
To gear up...no further choice.

VISA card statements for last year
Peel off the laser printer
Revealing in precise measure and chronological order
Our last year's sojourns together.

Snowbirds in Florida last winter,
Only happened once, but how rich!
Each break-camp and move of the pickup and pull-behind trailer
Chronicled—just follow the money trail.

Waves of tears as each entry
Brings memories of Spanish-moss-lined canals,
Manatees in warm springs,
Ospreys gorging on fish on Honeymoon Island,
Plovers combing the St. Augustine shores,
Fish 'n Chips with Poh-Boys washed down with Peroni,
Walks hand in hand in the moonlight.
Fewer tears of regret, now more thank you for what we have shared.

Snowbirds together, only once, but how grand!
So go the paper trails that give witness to a great love.

PILGRIMAGE

Brother, how kind of you
To chauffeur me in my new but lonely RV
On a sojourn missed not once, but twice
To the biggest item
On our bucket list:
The Grand Canyon.

Sister, how dear of you
To open your house to us for those days
As I traced the paths through the Garden of the Gods
Walked now so long ago—you and my family.
You will be the first to share these written thoughts of
The Grand Canyon.

Oh my God! Who can ever take in
This yawning mass of endless colors!
The gaping chasm that spans for miles;
The tiny silver line below hiding spring rapids.
The chatter of visitors broken by the croak
Of a fat raven in the pine above.
Too many tourists more interested
In catching a bit of themselves in a selfie with
The Grand Canyon.

A sudden cool breeze rises up the cliff
Hitting my cheek as like unto a kiss.
"Is that you, my dear?"
My eyes well with tears;
No space for a melt-down in this melee.
"Brother, let's go home!
My pilgrimage is done."
I'll say our goodbye to
The Grand Canyon.

REST

The weeks before and after you were gone
Were days of inexpressible angst and activity.
Family and friends coming and going
Sharing their love and concern to me and to you,
At the end of the day I would crash and rest,
In our bed once again, yet soon alone.

The exotic sea-cruise to the Barrier Reef,
Along the Down Under and on to Bali
Was a forced time of reflection and rest,
Preparing me for the days ahead.
And then the memorial service--
Did I include everyone in the thank-yous?
After the casseroles stopped arriving came reality:
I am truly alone to rest, but sleep evades me.

Now exactly nine months since we parted
I am strong enough to venture out alone
To places we have called home.
To Madagascar and wander the beaches
And the corridors of the hospital I once directed.,
Then Tanzania, our part in creating a dream.
I pace the halls of our former homes
Full of ghosts of times together.
Unstructured time for rest and reflection.

Now retired I have the luxury of doing
Little of nothing but rest.
These are precious times as I finally
Take the time to rest in our Lord.

A dear Tanzanian leader prayerfully asked me today,
"What Kingdom work awaits you?"
This question not yet answered, I rest,
To gain the inner strength for that new road
Leading only He knows where, yet
With the promise that it will be for good.

A NEW SONG

On final approach to Tolagnaro, Madagascar,
First Lokaro Beach in view,
Then the lighthouse hill,
Over old Fort Dauphin town
Then Lebanon point,
The Boeing turns base leg
After Whale Point;
Like a Canada honker ready to light,
The flaps of the jet fight the draw
Of the rivermouth Vinanibe below.
The mains hit the rain-drenched runway
I'm home again.

Yet this arrival lacks the ache and tears
Of a long-delayed return to roots.
It seems now business the call.
Our pickup idles beyond the gate.

The morning rooster and mournful dog
Add weight to my morning iPad alarm.
The rain arrives on schedule
Eight to ten on time
Like a well-oiled clock.

This hotel with meetings morn to night,
My boarding school and Libanona beach
So close yet so far;
Is this my new song?
Or have I moved to just a different room?
What shall I sing in this estranged land?

BROKEN HEARTED

My heart is heavy
My soul weeps.
I am called again
To clean up a mess:
A village development project with issues
In Madagascar where we were sent
Years ago and I now see as
Our life's first bookend.

Is this task my life's final bookend,
Playing out near our first assignment?
Is this the town of our youth
Where I play out my last card?

Many a patient of mine
When losing their soul partner
Has given up the ghost
And died of a broken heart.

I feel brittle, so vulnerable,
Without you near to share and confide.
Do I have the strength now alone
As I had here before?
The task is as thankless
As the work of our first bookend years ago.
I am broken-hearted, incomplete
Without you by my side.

Then come the psalmist's words
Memorized so long ago
In this town of my youth:
"Why are you downcast, O my soul?
Why so disturbed within me?
Put your hope in God,
For I will yet praise Him, My Savior and my God!" Ps 42:11 NIV

GOODBYE TO LOVE

I'm back in Fort Dauphin--town of our youth.
The wind in my face
Off the ocean's whitecaps
Blowing the fluffy clouds
Across the very blue sky
Over the old Norfolk pine
Broken in half
From a hurricane years ago.

I close my eyes
To feel fifty years younger:
I see the smartly white-washed walls
Of our school and home.
We are at the harbor
Full of love and with the touch
Of your side to mine
Rushing my heart
As I give you the necklace
That now rests in our safe
Full of meaning left now to me.

I open my eyes
Only to now see moldy plaster,
Rusty roof tins,
Mangy dogs,
Scrawny chickens,
The rusty colored hair
Of the beggar children
Fighting for my attention.

My plane leaves in two hours,
I've not even seen Libanona beach
My meetings are done.
We crush through the exit door
Racing for unassigned and oversold seats.
The jet engines throw me back
Into my aisle seat.
The Fort Dauphin bay quickly recedes.
Is this another final goodbye?

MIDNIGHT TEASE

Three flights spanning airports MSP, CDG, TNR, FTU:
Minneapolis, Paris, Antananarivo, Fort Dauphin (Madagascar).
Twenty-four hours of flying south and east;
Any further and I would get lost in Antarctica.
Now I rest on the hotel's cliff,
Overlooking Libanona beach and reefs.
The half moon's light bright enough
To cast shadows on my bench and table.

The familiar rhythm of the waves' white wash
Flowing over the ancient reefs,
Lit by the flickering reflections of coastal lights.
They move with the never-ending ocean swells
Which over leagues of travel
Have found their final mark as they plunge their soul
Finally, on the pale Libanona beach below.

The moon's reflection on the Australian 'filao' pines,
Papaya fronds, hibiscus flowers, frangi-pangi stems
Leave wavy shadows on my path below,
Broken only by my flashlight's glow,
Guiding me around the pines' roots--
Knuckled and polished yet hard as stone;
Just waiting to give my feet another trip.

This hotel verandah is over the same spot
Where I sat with you forty-eight years ago;
Holding hands, but aching for much more.
Finally I fall asleep way past midnight's call;
The silence broken only by the endless surf below
And one insomniac dog's refrain.

I dream I hear your voice clear as day
Just in the next room!
I race around the corner to find you
Smiling at me so lovingly;
Looking as young as we were then.

We hug and kiss and I awake--
A precious Libanona midnight tease.

I flip on the bed-stand light,
Adjust the mosquito net to close a hole
Opened by my sleep's trashing.
My pen and pad are recording these words,
No rush..I have all night,
"Goodnight, my dear!"

ANNIVERSARY BLUES

Today is our oldest's birthday,
Then yesterday would be our anniversary.
Remember that one year I forgot our wedding date
While here on mission assignment in Madagascar?
My Manambaro mission hospital duties from morn till night...
Until the next morning--I froze--
I came to you in shame.
You just smiled and forgave.

Today is our oldest's birthday
Again, I am so busy putting out fires
In this Madagascar town of our youth
That our date has slipped my mind once again.
Yesterday would have been
Our first anniversary apart
And I forgot yet again! Yet this time
Some shame, no tears, just a wistful moment,
And on to another meeting.

Is this how it will be?
Is this the path I take?
Fewer tears, only rare chokes.
At least the wrenching grief of months ago
Seemed to give credence to our deep love.
What do I say now, dear heart?

WHEN THE COCK CROWS

The mosquito net carefully tucked and the pillow just so
I fall asleep in the bedroom we shared for five years
Back at Manambaro Hospital, Madagascar
Where we raised our three young ones
With the help of our nanny Elizabeta
Yet already thirty years ago.

I fall asleep at eight PM because what else is there to do
But to read a book and drop it half-page through.
I awake suddenly as the roosters crow their first calls:
At one thirty, then four, then finally five-thirty.
I awake after the third rooster crow,
And head to the bathroom, no water on tap, so what's new?
I'm still skilled at throwing water on my head with a cup
Just like we did thirty years ago.

Breakfast and supper are with the resident doctor couple next door,
However, lunch is prepared by dear yet aging Elizabeta,
A few bites, a banana, then I walk through our familiar kitchen.
I stroke the top of our round dining table in the verandah
Where we shared so many meals
Already thirty years ago.

I am drawn to the familiar sounds, crusty clothes, hats, and banter
Of the otherwise miserably poor patients at the hospital
Who smile as they recognize this former doctor;
I may be still as eager and impetuous,
Yet now gray-haired and rounder;
Not the thin, young missionary doctor of thirty years ago.

The operating room is as if frozen in time,
The operating light is the same, just a few cracks on the glass frame,
The floor tiles are the same worn off-white and green tiles,
Speckled with black stains and cracks;
In a bit tougher shape than thirty years ago.

Back at our house I walk the floors from room to room,
I trace each wall and cupboard, look out each window,
Sit on the same furniture and ache that we could
Sit down and read another story to our young ones,
Tuck them in bed, hear their prayers, then await the cock's first crow
As was our routine thirty years ago.

MIXED EMOTIONS

Early in the departure lounge,
Where we arrived in Madagascar
Thirty-three years ago,
I am a bit numb with 'mixed' emotions:
Joy and Happiness.

I open my computer screen
Only to find your smiling face.
It still seems strange to be traveling solo
So many journeys with you by my side:
A bit numb yet still a baseline sadness.

This trip more than all before,
I feel like the ugly American;
Strained goodbyes to church leaders,
Both parties full well knowing the reason why:
A feeling of betrayal, and better off
That I am gone.

Will this be my last goodbye?
Is this the answer to two generations of giving?
How shall we explain to those before us
Buried on yonder cemetery hill?
Why should it matter anyway?
It is no longer our work,
It never was, let it go!
Homeward bound, a deep sigh.

SOLITUDE

The peach shades on the horizon as the sun makes its entrance,
The silver rays from the moon showing through the night's sky,
The mournful morning call of the ring-necked dove,
Or the wail of bush-babies calling me out of my dreams;
In these moments of solitude
You commune still with me.

This extended journey to places we have shared,
So full of schedule and encounters,
Creating background noise
That only solitude can clear,
So that, in my heart of hearts,
I may hear you.

SILENCE

Hush, my dear John,
Be silent and listen!
You always talked too much anyway.
Hear me in the morning call of the bulbul.
Feel me with the caress of the morning breeze.
See me through the pied crow
Sailing on the updraft of Windy Heights.
Only in these silent moments may you
Join me in the communion of all creation!

Join me in the creative suffering
Where you, like me,
Will experience the wonder
And the beauty of all you see and meet.
We both were baptized into Him
Who suffered that we might live.
Be patient, my love, you are not far.
Listen, while in communion
He whispers, "Be still, and know that I am God!"

WAIT

The morning game drive is over,
Tea-time has come and gone;
Now resting on the Tarangire lodge verandah*
Overlooking the baking acacias
Tempered by the Tarangire river,
Trickling along in a silver stream
All resonating the theme of wait.

Awakened by lions' throaty growl
Early before first dawn's light;
No sleep after such a prelude, so
I took the time earlier than later
For my daily dose of Oswald Chambers**
With today's theme being 'wait'.

Gone the gut wrenching sobs,
No longer the panic of utter loss,
Well on the journey of grief ne'er before taken,
Not by choice, no GPS or map.
This morning there is no movement
Either in the thickets below or in the lodge.
Guests all out on game drives,
Dishes are being sorted for lunch,
Another hour of wait.

Tomorrow is another story,
I will ply yet another road we shared
To yet another station of our lives together,
Now to be seen in different light.
Dodoma of our dreams now nearly accomplished.
This project once ours, to review.
Your passion for landscaping
Now in fruition, a garden in the desert.
You no longer need wait, my dear
I below and you above, to see.

---

* www.tarangiresafarilodge.com
** Oswald Chambers, *My Utmost For His Highest*, Discovery House, 1992

EMAYANI MEMORIES

Arrival in a sisal field airstrip
By turboprop Coastal-Air flight.
Bumpy twenty-minute drive to the beach lodge*
Shaded by myriads of coconut palms.
Fine with coral sand paths
Caress my bare feet as I walk
On out to our Bungalow Ten.
But just me this time.

Curried fish supper, then Scrabble
Before off to sleep, mosquito net prepped.
New twist: 24/7 electricity!
Hermit crabs cruise the bungalow perimeter.
The sleep of the dead broken by
Five AM wail of the mullah down the beach.

Up before sunrise with my camera
To catch the peach glow of the sunrise.
Leisurely breakfast—choose your eggs and meat;
Mine always sausage and Spanish omelet
Tweaked with a touch of goat pepper.

First a dip in the warm shallows,
Shower, then a circle or two in the pool.
I walk the beach to WindyPop creek,
Showing the newbies the sites.
It's just not the same without you.
This is where we laid back, loved,
And shared quiet routines.

The rain came in torrents
The morning I am to leave.
Will the plane land? Will I catch my flight home?
By the time we reach the sisal field
The sky is broken cumulus with cleansed blue.
The turboprop appears a speck on final.
No worries, what will be will be.
This is Tanzania. I'll be back!

---

* www.emayanibeachlodge.com

FULL COURT PRESS

Ten years ago I stayed on
You returned home.
I, completing a project,
And you, caring for your marrow.
This, the first time apart ever for us,
For that long six months.

Running the border of the Dodoma property,
The early sun glistening on the sisal's dew,
Suddenly out of nowhere—full court press!
As if my guts on display I begin to wail.
My run stopped, all muscles taut.
I nearly scream a primeval shout,
The tears blur my vision, my eyeballs ache.
I am alone, no one to hear the pain,
All the better to let it all out, alone.

Now another six months since you have gone.
Yet not for a while this time, now for good.
Returning from travel away I awake early.
Jet lag allows me a jump on the morn.
Just the tick of the African olive-wood clock,
And the plaintive call of the robin in the maple.
I'm back in rhythm with morning devotions;
Grief manuals providing daily motivation.

Suddenly out of nowhere—full court press!
Again the guttural wrenching cry, sobs, jerks, chokes,
Clenched hands held high.
However, I'm not totally alone—neighbors a wall away.
My cries are like a muted trumpet,
All the better to let it all out alone.

THOSE EYES

Sitting in the Nairobi departure lounge
Sipping on a cold Fanta
Across the small café
Is a pair of inviting eyes.

Brown eyes of a red-head
Not too young and not too old
Obviously trying to engage
These blue eyes.

Years of politely disengaging,
As it has been definitely a taboo
For me, up to now,
To fix on any set of eyes
But you.

She orders a burger and fries.
I finish my Fanta
And take a walk around,
Choosing to leave those eyes behind.

HALF OF THE WHOLE

I've nearly completed this two-month sojourn,
The longest trip of my life.
Sitting at a Dublin fish 'n chips
Feeling quite homesick.
So much sensing I'm cruising
As half of the whole, missing you!

Today I've kissed the Blarney Stone
To prove to my Irish-rooted sister-in-law
I've done my tourist duty.
Part of my whirlwind tour of Ireland
With my new Irish family:
My first cousin married to a bonnie lass,
Their two sons, now call me Uncle John.
Strange still traveling without Auntie Joann,
As half of the whole.

Tomorrow, a full day set aside:
Trinity College, the Book of Kells,
The Guinness factory tour ending with a taste, of course;
Double-decker open-top bus city tour,
Yet, by now, what's another cathedral more or less?

Finishing this evening at Madigan's,
Quite the typical Irish pub,
Testing a pint of "Five Lamp" ale,
Ending with a shot of Jameson "Black Barrel" whiskey,
Yet, no one to come home to,
Feeling again this night but half of the whole.

As I sip this fine shot of whiskey,
My thoughts go back a day or two--
Old Ross Castle framed by ancient pines
With Killarney Lake in background;
Then throw in a handful of graceful swans,
With a tease of sun breaking through
The clouds caressing the national park mountains.

Are you in the winds across the waters?
Tears well in my eyes but the sobs are gone.

This two-month marathon trip started in Madagascar,
Then Tanzania, and on to France's Alsace-Lorraine.
Now I cool my heels in this Dublin bar.
Soon London, then the train to Edinburgh.
Finally flying home again with the dawning awareness
That I am nearly whole.

GUINEVERE

I grabbed our GPS today
Put in the address and who did I hear but
The voice of our Guinevere!

Streams of pleasant memories of
Two gray-haired snow birds in Florida
Led on their wintering way by
The voice of our Guinevere.

You always kept me on course;
I would fly, you would read the charts.
I would drive, you managed the maps.
I would plot, you would pray for grace.
So we would move on, led by
The voice of our Guinevere.

I am longer flying these days.
I numbly plot my RV travels at a frenetic pace.
Plodding ahead day to day.
Yet my course falters--
A solo gander blindly coursing the winds,
Calling to his mate who is never to return.
Left with only
The voice of our Guinevere.

MISSING CONVERSATIONS

How many times a day
Do I have a question for you?
How often do I wish
You could share my fancy pot of stew?
Now with the best camera I have ever had,
The bird shots are spectacular
Come see! But of course,
You are not here.

Yet even more profound
Are the questions of my heart.
We never talked how you would feel
If now I was to dare seek another love.

But wait! Your friend,
Your heart of hearts confidante,
Who shared your life of prayer,
She would surely know!
So in a way, I rest assured that
The answers from your heart
Extend beyond the veil.

SAW-TOOTH SLIDE

My first trip with my new companion
Has me amazed at simple things
That we had lost in slow but sure bites
Out of your once vigorous body,
During your long but slow decline
Much like a saw-tooth slide.

During a hike down a rocky path
I turned to give her a hand
Which she took only out of courtesy,
Commenting in my chivalry.
However, this had almost become instinct
To help you as you lost your strength
After one of those first saw-tooth dips.

A walk around Lake Nokomis
With my new love on a cold, brisk winter day
With our scarves protecting our faces
Icicles forming on our eyebrows.
How long had it been since we played in the snow
After your loss of circulation forced an end to this?
Another dip in your saw-tooth slide.

In fact, how long had it been
Since we had taken a hike
Up to Lookout Mountain?
Had it been two years or more my dear?
Instead of that hike the boys and I
Took you up the start of the Cascade trail
Using our brawn to scoot your wheelchair
To view the familiar falls;
Further down your saw-tooth slide?

I run my fingers through her sandy colored hair
Causing a smile to grow in her sleepy face.
How I remember caressing your hair
Which had all but disappeared
Before your last and final slide,
As you slipped peacefully out of my view, forever.

LIGHTER SHADOWS

After you were gone
You were still front and center
Of every event of every day,
Heavily shadowing any thought or memory of joy
Replaced by violent sobs,
After you were gone.

Since you've been gone
You were still beside me,
Still there but not a pressing preface
To all as I plodded on.
The months move on
Yet now the sobs are reserved
For those intense connections
Such as singing the Sanctus at Communion—now alone;
My eyes there filling with tears
Replacing the sobs
Since you've been gone.

How long has it been?
My creative writing is no longer a daily urge.
Does this lack of intensity mean something less?
I have hung your memorial picture
Front and center of my desk
For fear I am losing those longings,
Those feelings we shared so intensely.
How long has it been?

What is through this next strange door?
It's scary but I must admit a bit exciting!
I went through yesterday with nary a tear.
I admit my eyes wander from time to time.
I came across the Ektachrome of the two of us
Three years old in the grass together.
The picture over time has lost its intense reds
Instead now capitalized by its tones of blue.
Our past is fading into lighter shadows.
I hear a definitive thunk behind me
As I pass through this strange new door.

MARGIN AND SANITY

While walking through life together
I constantly needed to work on margin,
That parceling out of time
Where I could leave work behind
And cultivate the precious love we had.

How to measure this margin, this sanity?
As I shared with you many a time
My barometer of margin and sanity
Would be the time spent on passions.
For me, outside of our love it would be
Flying and music.

Our last year together
Became one of survival,
That was true for the both of us.
Margin and sanity took a back seat.
If we both survived the day
We considered that a success.
My piano sat quiet,
The Piper Cherokee still in the hanger
No flying and little music.

Now that you are gone
What shall I say about margin and sanity?
Do the same measures apply?
If so, I am in a sad state:
Still the Piper awaits the leap into the air,
Piano music lays stacked beside a quiet keyboard.
I owe it to you and me to again create margin,
A bit more sanity in my life.
With effort I will soar again,
I sang a new song at the last funeral,
Did you clap for me, my dear?

PART THREE: A NEW DAWN

"You've got to get up every morning,
And show the world all the love in your heart!"
Carol King

"The people who walked in darkness have seen a great light;
Those who dwelt in a land of deep darkness,
On them has light shined."
Isaiah 9: 2

"Cast your burdens on the Lord,
And He will sustain you."
Psalm 55: 22

"There's beauty in that silver singin' river
There's beauty in that sunset in the sky,
But none of these and nothin' else can touch the beauty
That I remember in my true love's eyes.
Yes and only if my own true love was waitin'
And if I could hear her heart a-softly poundin,'
Yes, only if she was lyin' by me
Then I'd lie in my bed once again."
Bob Dylan

SPRING FEVER

Another early morning awakening,
Even before you, my robin friend.
Showered, fed, and in my right mind,
Even before the sun rises over the newly leaved poplars.
No cathartic wailing this morning
'Cause my heart is restless,
Finally eager for what is in store
On this fine spring day.

They warned me not to make
Any big decisions for at least a year.
I have broken that rule,
I'm closing on a condo,
Leaving this apartment of ghostly goodbyes,
Trying out somewhere new.
You remember the place,
We looked at it once.
Like our Dodoma weaver bird
Making a nest for his mate;
Once completed she would come and decide
If it was fine, or else tear it down.
I don't care, 'cause my heart is restless
On this fine spring day.

THE GARDEN

It is the third day of spring
March fury dropping a layer of snow
On your garden, just awakening.
Chives peek through the mulch,
Brave crocuses will soon give a thumbs-up to the tulips.

With the bright sun melting the white away
The robins are back!
Four fat ones awaiting the emerging worms
Seeking the warmth of the sun-soaked soil.

The pail of garden tools is waiting
Your eager hands to plant your nursery finds.
Each spring I would tolerate the money spent
On annuals that were just that!

Oh, that I could take a nursery run
With you, my hopeful gardener.
The nuthatch is back at the garden feeder.
Time to tend to the living.

THE FREEZER

Digging through the freezer
I've got to clean out this mess!
Zip-lock bags of past vegan treasures
Many precede your demise.
Two bags of all bran muffins
Sporting freezer crystals,
Another few of cooked squash.

Then what is this?
Gray-brown freeze in snap top,
Is it your mom's famous soup?

All your clothes and shoes are gone,
Your familiar scent long since disappeared.
But the aroma of our meals together
Par hazard, wait for me
All in Zip-Lock bags packed for two.

TALK

Early morning bathroom calls
I would return and snuggle in,
My front to your back,
You in half sleep would say,
"Good-morning, dear."
Wanting to talk I would tease you awake,
My finger lightly running the ridges of your ear,
A sure erotic trigger of yours forever.
A slight shiver, goose-bumps, then an embrace.
We would talk.

Early morning bathroom calls
I return to an empty bed and snuggle in,
My front to your lonely pillow,
The only sound is the pre-dawn call
Of our joyful robin chiming in the morn.
I grab your pillow for something to hold.
I greet you, "Good morning, dear."
I talk—somehow it feels right and good.
"Do you hear me?"
It's good I'm alone—talking to myself.
It's OK to talk:

"I saw an Eastern bluebird out in the ball field yesterday!
I must mark it down in our bird book.
The last one I saw was with you in Wesley Chapel."

SWEET SADNESS

This year's lilacs are quickly wilting,
A full year since you posed
For the last picture.
The lilac blooms
Frame your beautiful hair
That I would feel for the last time.

Now all I have is this memory
In the screenshot that greets me each day:
You smiling back at me
Your face full of love and acceptance
Fearlessly diving into ruin.

As the lilacs have faded,
So also my wrenching sobs.
I now ponder your face in that photo
And can now smile back
With nary a tear,
Yet filled with a lingering longing
And a sweet sadness.

BETTER THAN NEW

Eleven months since you passed into paradise.
Today I heard Luke's gospel story of the ten lepers healed:
The gnarled hands and feet of all ten lepers
Now restored to baby-skin smooth—better than new.
Yet only one with a heart full of praise returns to thank his Savior.
All ten healed but only the one's faith has saved him.
Only the long-suffering heart and soul of this one man
Is now filled with thanksgiving and saving grace.

Yes, eleven months since you passed into paradise.
My once blinding grief has now been graciously lifted.
The awful specter of your death by grace now replaced
With a clearer and sweeter vision of you:
Singing praises at your Savior's feet;
Your frame and very marrow now fully restored to better than new!

Eleven months of loneliness is soon over
As today I give my heart to a new love!
Rejoice with me this happy day!
I once again have a kindred spirit, a helpmate, a moral compass;
Once again, one to caress and share warmth.
Rejoice with me as once again I am whole.

So now, I RELEASE YOU with tears of joy to the
embrace of your Savior.
I am healing and, although my love for you will never end,
I can now bid you adieu
In the assurance that you are now not only healed,
But in a love that is infinitely better than new!

CROSSING THE LINE

"Forsaking all others, till death do us part."
Your dear friend and I share a gala affair,
A bit awkward for our friends and us.
You and I never talked this over:
Would you give me permission to share
An intimate moment with someone other than you?
How do I hug when my widowed friend is not you
Yet should be accepted as so?

We share a full moon shining over Lake Nokomis.
We both ponder quietly how it feels
To share this moment with another—alone—no words
Me, not with you—and she, not with him.

Is it OK, my dear, to dare to love again?
A very tentative kiss goodnight
And I have crossed the line.

NOW COMFORTABLE FREEDOMS

Less guilty of leaving the bed half made,
Tonight's dishes now easily wait the morning.
Saturday's former *au rigueur* cleaning routine
Now awaits the visible dust because it
"Ain't nobody's business if I do!"*

Led Zeppelin's "Stairway to Heaven" belts out at '30' volume,
Still in my jammies at ten AM.
Google calendar reports, "You have no scheduled events today."
My morning walk will have to wait till sundown 'cause it
"Ain't nobody's business if I do!"

Physician recruiters hound me with 'marvelous' ops like
"Come to Kansas and live it up!"
Each DELETE leads me further
From my other lifetime identity.
Shall this new author drop the 'MD' in his title?
"Ain't nobody's business if I do!"

Our juicer is long gone
Vegan delights are now complemented generously with
Pastrami on rye or marinated sirloin tips
Washed down with a 'Nordeast' or 'Pascual Toso Malbec' 'cause it
"Ain't nobody's business if I do!"

---

* Billie Holiday's song of the same name.

MISSING CONVERSATION

Remember when we cared for
The missionary mother gravely ill?
Her words of instruction that if she were to die
That her husband should marry so and so.
She recovered and they still are married happily
Years down the turnpike.

How is it we never broached this subject?
What should the one of us left behind do about marriage
If one of us were to pass?
Was it that, if either of us were to bring up the subject,
That whoever brought it up would in effect
Be in some way less faithful to our great love?

You are now gone and I am left alone
To answer this great question alone.
I have toiled hard on this work of grief
Now shy of one year.
Looking at your picture above my desk
Your generous and selfless loving smile
Permeates the room with perfume.
At first view I would shake with sobs of grief.
But now more like a quiet sadness mixed with real joy
For all the loving memories we shared together.

No, I am no longer alone to answer this question.
I have fallen in love for a second time.
With the benediction of your soul-mate speaking for you,
And the blessings of your extended family and closest friends;
It is they who have filled in our missing conversation
And the resounding answer is YES!

"One great love begets another."—Anonymous

HOLIDAY BLUES

The first Christmas without you
Barely six weeks from when you passed
Forced me going through the motions
For the sake of our children, not particularly me.
Christmas decorations at a minimum
No tree—too painful to hang
The treasured tree ornaments
A ritual in its own right.

This second Christmas without you
In a new place with a new love.
The tree, although a miniature, is hung with a few ornaments.
The stockings again decorate yet another mantle
Guarded by our nutcracker soldier.
The two youngest have chosen to celebrate with their closest friends,
Far from here--one in Virginia, the other in Maine.
Only our oldest and my new love with me this year.
We share the Christmas story, carols, Scandinavian sweets--
Old rituals mixed with a new and a certain joy.

Our African violet gave up the ghost
This last day of the year.
I have tried to nurse it along since you left without avail.
I said goodbye to this now lifeless plant
And will plant a new flower this coming spring.

GRIEF TO GRATITUDE

Your beautiful smile once again adorns my screensaver,
Your Friar Tuck mascot and college bob.
Our picture is back up on the wall.
No longer evoking jerking sobs
These memories now warm my healing heart.
Full of gratitude for the great love we shared,
Tears of rejoicing as we smile—together.

Time to take your carefully-created family albums
Off the storage room shelves,
And revel again in a lifetime of living.
Energy now to scan and pass on to our children
The record of this great love—with gratitude.

WHAT WAS US? WHAT IS ME?

Growing up together
And then nearly forty-two years married
Literally had us fused at the hip.
Over time what was ourselves
Became molded into what was us.

You are now gone—but are you?
Your picture is on the wall
Smiling down at me.
Yet now there has been a surgical excision.
My hip is disjointed—no longer fused
As only half of what was there.
It has become now what is me.

I have wandered five countries
Since you have gone.
My traveling lust is still there.
However, I don't have you to laugh with me,
To share the new bird calling in the bush.
Our travels together are ended,
The road is left to what is me.

At first, I didn't care for what was left.
I have had difficulty rediscovering what is only me.
Slowly, but surely, I am coming out of my pity party.
With quiet reflection and prayer I have come to the truth
As I ask God, "What is me?"
He has gently reminded me,
'You have been bought with a price,
You are precious in my sight,
You are and have always been mine!"

THE LONG GOODBYE

Your gut wrenches joined by sweat and a touch of nausea
As you hear the words, "Your cancer is back."
Unspoken is the reality that this will be the beginning of
The long goodbye.

Your response: a valiant fight.
We will beat this thing!
Uncountable internet searches for the newest hope
Makes you more up to date than most clinicians.
You have beaten the odds by many years.
Yet, now each failed attempt of a cure
Returns the unspoken thought of your passing.

My dear friend, I join you now this early hour.
The agony of the imminent causes my pen to move.
How is it that our creative moments come
While facing yet another long goodbye?

On our way to visit you, now in hospice,
We had stopped in for a graduation party,
For us septuagenarians, an increasingly rare event.
We commented how, in our present stage of life
Obituaries now scanned for those we might know.
Our gatherings are now more often
Memorial services of dear friends and family.

However, you and I know yours was coming for a long time.
You, in warrior mode, in fierce denial to the end.
Yet, I the seasoned practitioner over that same time
Only awaiting the call announcing your final goodbye.

I thought this collection of poems of grief were finished
Only to awake some years later in the early hours.
My pen now trying to catch up to my flood of emotion.
Again I put on the breastplate from my Savior
To gird myself in preparation for the finality of this
Another expected long goodbye.

Unbeknownst to me that same early morning awakening
Was the call of your soul to your Savior.
The words of the hymn "When Peace Like a River"
Flooded me with comfort till we got the word that
We are again one dear friend less.
You honored me with your death wish that we and another dear friend honor your memory with the gift of music.

Your memorial: my prayer that our rendition of "Peace Like a River" be acceptable as an offering.
Your chosen Psalm 121 comforts us,
Assuring each of us that that we are not alone!
"He who keeps Israel will neither slumber nor sleep."
Echoes of beloved hymns sung to our Savior's glory
Bring me again to tears of joy.
The words of commitment over your urn seem a bit belated.

You have already crossed over Jordan,
You have heard the trumpet sound,
Your faith is now indeed sight,
Your clouds rolled back like a scroll,
Your sonnets now flow through the river of grace
As you have entered into His pure light.
Finally, you may cast your crown at His feet
Praising Him timelessly face to face!

What a fitting bookend and closure to this pen's flow.
My own journey can now continue in deeper courage
As I walk in time and grace to my own final long goodbye.

ABOUT THE AUTHOR

John Toso, MD is a retired family physician. He has had a varied career—working in two rural Minnesota communities as a family practitioner, running a missionary hospital in southern Madagascar, and later designing and acting as project director for Dodoma Christian Medical Center Trust, a faith-based hospital in central Tanzania. He is a graduate of Concordia College, Moorhead, Minnesota, the University of Minnesota Medical School, a diplomate of the American Society of Tropical Medicine and Hygiene, a Bush Medical Fellow, and graduate of the first cohort of the University of Saint Thomas Physician Leadership Program.

Having grown up as 'MK's (missionary kids) in Madagascar, John and his now deceased wife Joann were well positioned to serve, first in Madagascar and later in Tanzania. They have three grown children and two grandchildren.

John's first wife of forty-two years—Joann—suffered with a myeloproliferative disease for seventeen years, finally succumbing to her illness in November of 2015. John has since remarried to Janet Johnshoy, longtime friend of the family. They revel in the role of grandparents and enjoy birding and travelling.

This is Dr. Toso's second book. His first—Windows On The Soul, an autobiographical work of missionary medicine in Madagascar—will soon be re-published in a second edition with the tentative title of Windows On Global Health.

Along with his writing Dr. Toso is a founding member and regular volunteer at Global Health Ministries, Fridley, Minnesota—a grassroots charitable organization supporting Lutheran healthcare organizations worldwide, which he helped create in 1987.